KINGS & QUEENS

OF ENGLAND
...and how they got there...

By

TONY THISTLEWOOD

(Third Edition)

Author

A.W. (Tony) THISTLEWOOD
FCA FGIA FCIS

Website:

tonythistlewood.com

Fiction:

Caistor Parsons: The Gingerbread Man

Stealing Tomorrow's Thunder

The Little Tin Box

The Oxford Photograph

Non-fiction:

Kings & Queens of England
...and how they got there

CONTENTS

PART 1
LONGEST REIGNING ROYAL HOUSES

(1) **PLANTAGENET** 1216-1485 (269 years)

(2) **HANOVER** 1714-1901 (187)

(3) **TUDOR** 1485-1603 (118)

(4) **WINDSOR** 1917- current (101 years to 2018)

(5) **STUART** 1603 -1649,1660-1694, and
1702-1714 (95)

(6) **NORMANDY** 1066 -1135 (69)

(7) **ANJOU** 1154 -1216 (62)

(8) **BLOIS** 1135 -1154 (19)

(9) **SAXE-COBURG & GOTHA** 1901-1917 (16)

(10) **ORANGE-NASSAU** 1694 -1702 (8)

NICKNAMES OF MONARCHS
from 1066

House of Normandy:

William I – the Bastard, the Conqueror

William II – Rufus (the red)

Henry I – Beauclerc or Beauclerk, Lion of Justice

House of Anjou:

Henry II – Curtmantle (short cloak), Lion of Justice, or Fitzempress (inferring that Henry was the illegitimate son of Empress Matilda)

Edward I – Langshanks (long legs), The Hammer of the Scots.

John – Soft-Sword or Lackland (without land) because John lost Anjou to the French.

Richard I – the Lionheart.

House of Plantagenet:

Henry IV – Bolingbroke. Henry was born in Bolingbroke Castle, Lincolnshire.

Richard III – Crookback. Like Robert Cecil, Richard suffered from scoliosis or curvature of the spine.

House of Tudor:

Henry VIII – Old Coppernose.

Cardinal Thomas Wolsey reduced the amount of gold and silver in coins to save money. Over time, the metal of the raised areas of a coin, including Henry's nose, wore off exposing the copper colour beneath.

Mary I – Bloody Mary

> Mary had nearly 300 Protestants executed for their alleged part in the attempt to place Lady Jane Grey on throne instead of her.

Elizabeth I – Gloriana, the Virgin Queen, Good Queen Bess

Jane – the Nine Days Queen.

House of Stuart:

James I/VI – the Vain, the Wisest Fool in Christendom.

Charles I – the Martyr

Charles II – the Merry

House of Orange:

William IV – the Sailor King

House of Hanover:

George III – the Farmer or Farmer George

George IV – the Prince of Whales

Victoria – Mrs Brown

House of Saxe-Coburg & Gotha

Edward VII – the Uncle of Europe

ABBREVIATIONS AND GLOSSARY

c.	about (Latin: *circa*)
d.s.p.	died *sine prole* (without issue)
d.s.p.s.	died *sine prole superstite* (without surviving issue)
ibid.	in the same place (Latin: *ibidem*)
q.v.	for which see (Latin *quod vide*). A cross reference often followed by a page number
r.	reigned
s.	surviving
s.p.	without issue (Latin *sine prole*)
s.p.m.s.	without surviving male issue (Latin *sine prole mascila superstite*)
Heir apparent:	The next person in a line of succession who cannot be replaced without a change to the rules of succession.
Heir presumptive:	The next person in a line of succession but who may be replaced by a subsequent event such as the birth of someone with a superior claim.
Salic Law:	Salic Law takes its name from *Lex Salica* being the codification of the law of the Salian Franks dating back to the fifth century. It developed in a mixture of the Latin, German and Dutch languages

and encompassed civil and criminal law and the law of inheritance. Its influence eventually impacted statute law throughout Europe.

Titulus Regus: Latin: *Royal Title*. An Act of Parliament passed in 1484 declaring that Edward IV's marriage was invalid and that his children, Edward V and Prince Richard, were therefore illegitimate and incapable of inheriting the crown.

PART 2

PRIMOGENITURE AND COUSINSHIP

FORMS OF PRIMOGENITURE

Primogeniture is the inheritance of titles and estates by the firstborn. It is an important element of Precedence as eventually codified in the *Precedence Act 1539*. Unfortunately, over the years, different interpretations of primogeniture have not only caused confusion but also wars. The various methods adopted are summarised below, and the abbreviations are used throughout this book.

1. M-PC (Male-preference Cognatic primogeniture)

> This commonly used method permits a female to inherit but only in the absence of the deceased monarch's living brothers or living sons of deceased brothers.

2. FC (Full Cognatic (absolute) primogeniture)

> The eldest child succeeds regardless of gender. In 2013, it was decreed that henceforward only the Full Cognatic method of primogeniture would be used for determining succession to the crown in the UK.

3. SL (i)) (Agnatic - Salic law - primogeniture)

> Only inheritance through the male line by the eldest son, then by younger sons, then by elder brothers, and so forth, is allowed. Female inheritance is not permitted.

4. SL (ii) (Semi-Salic Law (ii))

This version permits the sons of women to inherit but not women themselves.

5. SL (iii) (Semi-Salic Law (iii))

Women can inherit but only on the extinction of all patrilineal male descendants.

6. AS (Agnatic Seniority primogeniture)

AS is strict patrilineal inheritance to the extent that a monarch's younger brothers take precedence over the monarch's own children.

Of the forty-one monarchs that have reigned since and including William I in 1066, a substantial majority (76%) have done so by at least one, or both, of the *Male-preference Cognatic primogeniture* method (M-PC) and/or the *Full Cognatic (absolute) primogeniture* method (FC).

The charts in Part 3 of this book show the primogeniture method(s) used, from William I to Elizabeth II, and what might have happened had other available methods been adopted.

But first a word about...

COUSINSHIP

A cousin is a child of an aunt or uncle, of course. Well, that only gives the first degree of cousinship i.e. a first cousin. There are second, third, fourth, and so on, cousins; in other words, there are *degrees* of cousinship.

And it doesn't end there: after you have sorted out the degree of cousinship, you must consider the generation gap, if any, that exists between the cousins. This is stated as "times removed" and can affect any degree of cousinship.

You can calculate both the *degree* of cousinship and the *generation gap* (times removed), by applying the following simple steps:

1. For each cousin, count the number of grandparents and great-grandparents back to and including the grandparent that is common to both.

2. If the two numbers are different, the lower one gives the *degree* of cousinship i.e. first or second cousin. If the numbers are the same then obviously that number is the degree of cousinship.

3. If the two numbers are different, however, by deducting the lower from the higher you get the *generation gap* – the times removed number.

Just to make this crystal let us look at the relationship that existed between Edmund Mortimer, 5th Earl of March, and his wife, Anne Stafford, *before* they were married (see Part 3 – House of Plantagenet 3).

	Edmund Mortimer	Anne Stafford
Parent	Roger Mortimer	Anne Plantagenet of Woodstock
1. Grandparent	Philippa Plantagenet Countess of Ulster	Thomas Woodstock 1st Duke of Gloucester
2. Great-grandparent	Lionel of Antwerp, 1st Duke of Clarence	**Edward III**
3. Great-great-grandparent	**Edward III**	

The common grandparent was **Edward III**

The count-back of grandparents to the common grandparent gives:

Edmund 3 – Anne 2

The lower of these numbers (2) means that Edmund and Anne were *second cousins*.

The difference between the two numbers (1) represents the generation gap between the cousins.

Therefore, Edmund and Anne were *second cousins once removed*.

PART 3

KINGS & QUEENS of ENGLAND
Their Family Trees...and how they got there

THE HOUSE OF NORMANDY

Two years before his death on 5 January 1066, Edward the Confessor promised the crown of England to William, Duke of Normandy. Harold Godwinson, however, claimed that Edward recanted this promise on his deathbed and offered the crown to him instead. William insisted that Edward's promise to him took precedence and invaded England to press his claim. What followed was one of the bloodiest battles ever fought on English soil.

1066 – 14 October – **The Battle of Hastings**
In fact, the battle took place in East Sussex about 7 miles (11kms) from Hastings.

The Belligerents

The Anglo-Saxon King Harold Godwinson
Versus
William, Duke of Normandy

Harold was killed late in the day and only then was a decisive victory for the Normans assured. The Duke of Normandy was crowned William I of England on Christmas Day 1066, and the modern method of numbering monarchs starts with him.

HOUSE OF NORMANDY – Family Tree
(Offspring are inset below their parents)

William I (The Conqueror)
[r.1066-1087]

b.c.1028 d.1087
m. Matilda of Flanders, Duchess of Brabant d.1083

> (1 of 9+) Robert Curthose
> b.c.1051 d.1133/4
>
> (3) **William II**
> [r.1087-1100] b.c.1056 d.1100 d.s.p.
>
> (6) **Henry I**
> [r.1100-1135] b.c.1068 d.1135
> m.(i) Matilda of Scotland
>
>> (i of iii+) **Matilda**
>> [r.1141-1148 (disputed)]
>> b.c.1101/2 d.1167
>> m.(i) Henry V, Holy Roman Emperor d.s.p.1125
>> m.(ii) Geoffrey Plantagenet, 5th Count of Anjou
>> (For offspring see House of Anjou)
>
> (9) Adela
> b. unkn d.1136/37
> m. Stephen II, Count of Blois
> (For offspring see House of Blois below)

...and how they got there...
(For details of types of Primogeniture see Part 2)

(1) **William I** r.1066-1087

> Succeeded to the crown by the right of conquest at the
> Battle of Hastings 14th October 1066.
> Crowned 25th December 1066

(2) **William II** r.1087-1100 d.s.p. (second son of William I)

> Succeeded to the crown by: **M-PC, SL (i)**

Robert Curthose, eldest son of William I, should have succeeded William I as King of England. However, William gave Normandy to Robert and England to his second son, William II. Clearly, the Norman king still considered Normandy more of a prize than England. This succession did not follow any of the normal rules of primogeniture.

Other unsuccessful candidates:

FC

William I had five or six daughters; however, their birthdates are unknown, and therefore it is unclear who would have succeeded under this method.

(3) **Henry I** r.1100-1135 d.s.p.

(younger brother of William II)

Succeeded to the crown by usurpation:

When William II (William Rufus) was killed in a hunting accident (allegedly) his younger brother, Henry I (Beauclerc), *who just happened to be around at the time of the said accident,* seized the crown before his elder brother, Robert Curthose (see (a) above), managed to return from Normandy. Robert was militarily and politically incompetent and renounced his claim to the throne in the Treaty of Alton (1101). He spent the last twenty years of his life imprisoned in Devizes and Cardiff Castles.

HOUSE OF BLOIS – Family Tree
(Offspring are inset below their parents)

Adela, Countess of Blois (from House of Normandy)

> **Stephen**
> [r.1135-1154] b.c.1094 d.1154
> m. Matilda of Boulogne
> (All Stephen's children were illegitimate and therefore incapable of inheriting the crown)

... and how he got there...
(For details of types of Primogeniture see Part 2)

(1) **Stephen** r.1135-1154 (Nephew of Henry I)

> Succeeded to the crown by usurpation:
> Other unsuccessful candidates:

M-PC and SL (i)

> The next male in line was Stephen's elder brother, William Count of Sully known as William the Simple, which probably says it all. Stephen usurped the crown from his brother and his cousin, Matilda [ibid.]

FC

> Matilda, the eldest legitimate child of Henry I and named by him as his heir presumptive, could have and, in 1139-41, did try to legitimately succeed under this method (FC), but she was usurped by Stephen. Her son, Henry II, eventually succeeded Stephen because all Stephen's children were illegitimate and thus incapable of inheriting the crown.

SL (ii)

> William Sully and Stephen were sons of Adela, Countess of Blois, daughter of William I.

HOUSE OF ANJOU – Family Tree
(Offspring are inset below their parents)

Matilda
[r.1141-1148 (disputed)]
Countess of Anjou (from House of Normandy)

> **Henry II**
> [r.1154 -1189] b.1132/3 d.1189
> m. Eleanor of Aquitaine
>
> > (2 of 8) **Henry the Young King**
> > [r.1170-1183] b.1154/5 d.1183 s.p
> > m. Margaret of France
> >
> > (4) **Richard I**
> > [r.1189-1199] b.1157 d.1199 s.p.
> > m. Berengaria of Navarre
> >
> > (8) **John**
> > [r.1199-1216] b.1166 d.1216
> > m.(ii) Isabella of Angouleme
> >
> > > **Henry III**
> > > **(see House of Plantagenet below)**

... and how they got there...
(For details of types of Primogeniture see Part 2)

(1) **Henry II** r.1154-1189 (1st Cousin once removed to Stephen)

> Succeeded to the crown by: **M-PC, FC, SL (i)**
> Henry II was the eldest child of Matilda and
> Geoffrey Plantagenet, Count of Anjou. Thus, Henry
> II was the first King of England to have the surname

'Plantagenet'. However, *The House of Plantagenet* is now considered to start with Henry III, while kings Henry II to John are known as *The House of Anjou* to reflect the fact that those monarchs were kings of a wider part of Europe and not just kings of England.

(2) **Henry the Young King** r.1170-1183 (son of Henry II)

Co-ruler with his father, Henry II, in the Capetian tradition.

Because he pre-deceased his father, this Henry is not counted in the numerical sequence of monarchs. His elder brother, William, died before Henry was born.

(3) **Richard I** r.1189-1199 (younger son of Henry II)

Succeeded to the crown by: **M-PC, FC, SL (i)**

(4) **John** r.1199-1216 (younger brother of Richard)

Succeeded to the crown by: **M-PC, FC, SL (i), AS**

HOUSE OF PLANTAGENET – Family Tree (1)
Henry III to Edward III – 1216 to 1377
(Offspring are inset below their parents)

John (from House of Anjou)
[r.1199-1216] b.1166 d.1216
m.(ii) Isabella of Angouleme

> **Henry III** [eldest child]
> [r.1216-1272] b.1207 d.1272
> m. Eleanor of Provence
> Henry III was only 9 years old when he succeeded his
> father, King John. Henry's regents during his minority
> were William Marshall, 1st Earl of Pembroke, (1216-1219)
> followed by Hubert de Burgh, 1st Earl of Kent, (1219-
> 1227).
> In 1215, Henry III's daughter, Margaret, married
> Alexander III, King of Scotland.
>
> > **Edward I** [eldest child]
> > [r.1272-1307] b.1239 d.1307
> > m.(ii) Margaret of France
> > m.(i) Eleanor of Castile
> >
> > > **Edward II** [eldest son]
> > > [r.1307-1327] b.1284 d.1327
> > > m. Isabella of France
> > >
> > > > **Edward III** [eldest son]
> > > > [r.1327-1377] b.1312 d.1377
> > > > m. 1328 Philippa of Hainault d.1369
> > > > Issue: 5 sons
> > > > (see House of Plantagenet (2)
> > > > below)

HOUSE OF PLANTAGENET – Family Tree (2)
Edward III to Henry VI – 1327 to 1471
(Offspring are inset below their parents)

Edward III (from House of Plantagenet (1))
[r.1327-1377] b.1312 d.1377
m.1328 Philippa of Hainault d.1369

> (1 of 5) Edward Prince of Wales (The Black Prince)
> b.1330 d.1376
>
>> **Richard II**
>> [r.1377-1399] b.1367 d.1400 s.p.
>> m.(i) Anne of Bohemia d.1394
>> m.(ii) 1396 Isabelle de Valois
>>
>> Richard II's second wife, six-year-old Isabelle de Valois, was the sister of Catherine de Valois, widow of Henry V. Catherine subsequently married Owen Tudor with whom she had a son, Edmund, who became the father of the first Tudor monarch: Henry VII.
>
> 2) Lionel of Antwerp, 1st Duke of Clarence
> b.1338 d.1368
>
>> Philippa, Countess of Ulster
>> b.1355 d.1382
>> m. Edmund Mortimer, 3rd Earl of March
>>
>>> (i of v) Elizabeth Mortimer
>>> b.c.1386 d.1422
>>> m. Henry Percy (Hotspur)
>>>
>>>> Henry Percy, 2nd Earl of Northumberland
>>>> b.1392/3 k.i.b (St Albans) 1455
>>>> m. Eleanor Neville (Issue not shown)

(ii) Roger Mortimer, 4th Earl of March
b.1374 d.1398
m. Eleanor de Holland

> (2 of 4) Edmund, 5th Earl of March
> b.1391 d.1425 s.p.
> m.1408 Anne Stafford

(3) John of Gaunt, 1st Duke of Lancaster
b.1340 d.1399
m.1359 Blanche of Lancaster (his third cousin)

Henry IV
[r.1399-1413] b.1367 d.1413
m.(i) Mary de Bohun
Only three of John of Gaunt's many children with Blanche survived their father. Henry was the youngest of these and the only male.

Henry V
[r.1413-1422] b.c.1386 d.1422
m. 1420 Catherine de Valois
(Catherine's sister Isabella later married Richard II - see above)

> **Henry VI** (eldest child of 6)
> [r.1422-1461 and 1470-1471]
> b.1421 d.1471
> m. Margaret of Anjou
> Edward, their only child, was killed at the battle of Tewksbury in 1471.

(4) Edmund of Langley, 1st Duke of York
b.1341 d.1402
m.(1) Isabella of Castile

> (iii of iii) Richard, 3rd Earl of Cambridge

b.c.1375 ex.1415
m.c.1408 Anne Mortimer d.1421 – eldest child of
Roger Mortimer, 4th Earl of March (see above)
Richard's elder brother, Edward, d.s.p. at the
battle of Agincourt, 1415.

> (3 of 3) Richard, 3rd Duke of York (Richard
> of York)
> b.1411 k.i.b. (Wakefield) 1460
> m. Cecily Neville
> (**continued House of Plantagenet (3)
> below**)

(5) Thomas of Woodstock, 1st Duke of Gloucester
b1355 d.1397
m. Eleanor de Bohun
(Issue not shown because they did not directly
contribute to the succession of any monarch.)

HOUSE OF PLANTAGENET– Family Tree (3)
Edward IV to Richard III – 1461 to 1485
(Offspring are inset below their parents)

Richard, 3rd Duke of York (Richard of York)
(from Plantagenet 2)
b.1411 k.i.b. (Wakefield) 1460
m. Cecily Neville

(1) **Edward IV**
[r.1461-1470 and 1471-1483] b.1442 d.1483
m. 1464 (secretly) Elizabeth Woodville

(i) **Edward V**
[r. 9 April 1483 to 29 July 1483]
b.1470 d.1483?

Richard III imprisoned Edward V and his brother, Prince Richard, in the Tower of London because he believed them to be illegitimate and therefore incapable of inheriting the crown. The brothers were never seen again.

(ii) Prince Richard, Duke of York
b.1473 d.1483? (see Edward V above)

(iii) Elizabeth of York
b.1466 d.1503
m.1486 Henry Tudor (**Henry VII**)
(See House of Tudor below)

(2) Edmund, Earl of Rutland
b.1443 k.i.b. (Wakefield)1460

(3) George, 1st Duke of Clarence
b.1449 exec.1478

> m. 1469 Isabel Neville elder sister of Anne, wife of
> **Richard III**
>
> 4) **Richard III**
> [r.1483-1485] b.1452 k.i.b.(Bosworth Field)1485
> m. Anne Neville

Richard III's only son pre-deceased him and so Richard's death brought to an end both the Plantagenet line and the Mediaeval period of English history. His conqueror at Bosworth Field, Henry Tudor, succeeded him as **Henry VII**.

... and how the Plantanenets got there
(For details of types of Primogeniture see Part 2)

(1) **Henry III** r.1216-1272 (son of John)

> Succeeded to the crown by: **M-PC, FC, SL (i)**

(2) **Edward I** r.1272-1307 (son of Henry III)

> Succeeded to the crown by: **M-PC, FC, SL (i)**

(3) **Edward II** r.1307-1327 (son of Edward I)

> Succeeded to the crown by: **M-PC, SL (i)**
> Other unsuccessful candidates:
> **FC**
>> Margaret Duchess of Brabant, Lothier and Limburg (b.1275 d.1333), who was Edward II's elder sister, could have legitimately succeeded under this method.

(4) **Edward III** r.1327-1377 (son of Edward II)

> Succeeded to the crown by: **M-PC, FC, SL (i)**

Other unsuccessful candidates:
AS

Thomas Brotherton, 1st Earl of Norfolk and Edward II's younger brother (b.1300 d.1338), could have succeeded instead of Edward III under the AS method.

(5) **Richard II** r.1377-1399 (grandson of Edward III)

Succeeded to the crown by: **M-PC, FC, SL (i)**
Other unsuccessful candidates:
AS

John of Gaunt, 1st Duke of Lancaster, Edward III's oldest surviving son at the date of his death, could have succeeded Edward instead of Richard II under the Agnatic Seniority method because the crown would have passed to Edmund Langley on John of Gaunt's death and not to John's eldest son, Henry Bolingbroke. Richard II's claim was clearly much stronger than that of Henry, and it prevailed – for a time. There was no precedent for the AS method being used in isolation.

(6) **Henry IV** r.1399-1413 (1st cousin to Richard II)

Henry IV (Henry Bolingbroke) was the eldest child of John of Gaunt and the first monarch from the House of Lancaster. Henry probably argued that he was next in line after Richard II being his closest living male relative in terms of consanguinity; it obviously worked.

Succeeded to the crown by: **M-PC, SL (i)**
Other unsuccessful candidates:
Any of the following cousins/uncle of Henry IV (including Thomas of Lancaster - see (7) Henry V)

could legitimately have succeeded Richard II. This confusion of legitimate heirs was the origin of the Cousins' War *(War of the Roses).*

FC

Elizabeth Mortimer, wife of Henry (Hotspur) Percy, granddaughter of Lionel of Antwerp (Edward III's second son) and first cousin once removed to Henry Bolingbroke.

SL (ii)

Edmund Mortimer, nephew of Elizabeth Mortimer [ibid.], son of Roger Mortimer, great grandson of Lionel of Antwerp and first cousin twice removed to Henry Bolingbroke.

AS

Edmund of Langley, 1st Duke of York, fourth son of Edward III and uncle of Richard II and Henry Bolingbroke. All four of Edmund's brothers died before Richard II. The use of this method, however, would have been contentious because Richard II had no brothers and there was no precedent in England for Agnatic Seniority being taken back a generation as there was with the other versions of primogeniture. This later reinforced the Yorkist's claims.

(7) **Henry V** r.1413-1422 (son of Henry IV)

Succeeded to the crown by: **M-PC, FC, SL (i)**
Other unsuccessful candidates:

AS

Thomas of Lancaster, 1st Duke of Clarence, younger brother of Henry IV. A weak claim under Agnatic Seniority that was never pursued.

(8) **Henry VI** r.1422-1461 and r.1470-1471 d.s.p.s.
(son of Henry V)

Succeeded to the crown by: **M-PC, FC, SL (i), AS**

(9) **Edward IV** r.1461-1470 and r.1471-1483
(3rd cousin to Henry VI)

Succeeded to the crown by: **M-PC, FC**
Edward IV was a great-grandson of Edmund of
Langley, 1st Duke of York [ibid.] and, therefore, the
first monarch from the House of York. However,
either of Edward IV's siblings, Elizabeth of York or
Richard III, could legitimately have succeeded him.

(10) **Edward V** r.1483 d.s.p.s. (son of Edward IV)

Succeeded to the crown by: **M-PC, SL (i)**
Other unsuccessful candidates:
FC

Elizabeth of York, Edward V's elder sister could
have succeeded under this method. She eventually
became Queen consort to Henry VII.

AS

Richard III, being the last surviving younger brother
of Edward IV, could have succeeded under this
method. However, he chose the *Titulus Regus (see
glossary)* route and had Parliament declare
Edward's children illegitimate, thus confirming him
as king under the more normal primogeniture
methods **M-PC and SL**. This suggests that the
Agnatic Seniority method was considered unsafe
even then.

(11) **Richard III** r.1483-1485 (uncle to Edward V)

Succeeded to the crown by: **M-PC, SL (i), AS**
Richard III's claim looks strong enough on paper, but bear in mind that he had, by fair means or foul, eliminated his brother, Edward IV, and Edward's two young sons, Edward V and Prince Richard, before claiming the throne.

HOUSE OF TUDOR
Family Tree 1485 – 1603
(Offspring are inset below their parents)

Owen ap Maredudd ap Tudur
b.c.1400 d.1461
m.c.1430 Catherine de Valois (widow of **Henry V**)
b.1401 d.1436/7

> Edmund Tudor, 1st Earl of Richmond
> b.1430 d.1456
> m. 1455 Margaret Beaufort (the illegitimate great-great-granddaughter of Edward III)

> > **Henry VII**
> > [r.1485-1509] b.1457 d.1509
> > m.1485/6 Elizabeth of York (daughter of Edward IV) b1465/6 d.1502/3

> > > (1) Arthur
> > > b.1486 d.1502
> > > m.1501 Catherine of Aragon

> > > (2) Margaret
> > > b.1489 d.1541
> > > (see *Claim of Mary Queen of Scots*)

> > > (3) **Henry VIII**
> > > [r.1509-1547] b.1491 d.1546/7
> > > m. (see below for details of his six wives)

> > > (4) Mary
> > > b.1496 d.1533 (Note 5)
> > > (see *Claim of Lady Jane Grey*)

The Six Wives of Henry VIII
(Offspring are inset)

(1) **Catherine of Aragon**
m. (i) 1509 (annulled 23rd May 1533)
b.1485 d.1536
Catherine was the widow of Henry VIII's brother, Arthur.

> **Mary I**
> r. [1553 – 1558] b.1515/6 d.1558 s.p.
> m.1554 Philip II of Spain

(2) **Anne Boleyn** Marquess of Pembroke
m. (ii) 1533
b.c.1501 exec.1536
Anne Boleyn was the granddaughter of Thomas Howard, 2nd Duke of Norfolk.

> **Elizabeth I**
> [r.1558 – 1603] b.1533 d.1602/3
> (Never married)

(3) **Jane Seymour**
m. (iii) 1536
b.c.1508 d.1537
Jane Seymour was descended from Edward III through Lionel of Antwerp and Henry (Hotspur) Percy. She was a 5th cousin to Henry VIII and half-2nd cousin to Anne Boleyn.

> **Edward VI**
> [r.1547 – 1553] b.1537 d.1553)
> (Never married)

(4) **Anne of Cleves**

m. (iv) 1540 (annulled 1540)
b.1515 d.1557
Henry VIII's marriage to Anne of Cleves was not
consummated and was annulled in 1540.

(5) **Catherine Howard**

m. (v) 1540
b.c. 1518-25 exec.1542 d.s.p.

(6) **Catherine Parr**

m. (vi) 1543
b.c.1512 d.1548 d.s.p.

... and how the Tudors got there
(For details of types of Primogeniture see Part 2)

(1) **Henry VII** r.1485-1509

(3rd cousin once removed to Richard III)

Succeeded to the crown by right of conquest at the
Battle of Bosworth Field, 22nd August 1485.

Henry VII was the 3 times great-grandson of
Edward III. However, this was through the
illegitimate line of John of Gaunt and his mistress,
later 3rd wife, Katherine Swynford. Therefore,
Henry did not have a legal claim to the crown.

(2) **Henry VIII** r.1509-1547 (son of Henry VII)

Succeeded to the crown by: **M-PC, SL (i)**
Other unsuccessful candidates:
FC

Margaret Tudor, elder sister of Henry VIII, could legitimately have succeeded Henry VII instead of Henry VIII had she not married a foreigner, James IV of Scotland. They became the grandparents of Mary Queen of Scots. Henry VIII, however, later removed Margaret from the line of succession.

(3) **Edward VI** r.1547-1553 d.s.p.s age 15
(son of Henry VIII)

Succeeded to the crown by: **M-PC, SL (iii)**
Other unsuccessful candidates:
FC

Mary Tudor, elder half-sister of Edward VI, could legitimately have succeeded under this method. She later succeeded as Mary I.

(4) **Jane** r.1553 (9 days) d.s.p.s age 16
(1st cousin once removed to Edward VI)
Jane was a great-granddaughter of Henry VII. She was never crowned. *(See Claim of Lady Jane Grey)*

Succeeded to the crown by: **M-PC and SL (iii)**
In his will, Edward VI strangely overlooked Frances Brandon, Duchess of Suffolk and mother of Jane Grey, as heir presumptive naming her daughter, Jane, instead.
Other unsuccessful candidates:
SL (ii)

James V of Scotland had no legitimate sons, and so Henry Stuart, Lord Darnley, being a grandson of Margaret Tudor and her second husband, Archibald Douglas, Earl of Angus, considered that he had a claim under this method. Darnley was also married to his cousin, Mary Queen of Scots, who had a stronger claim being descended from Margaret's first husband, James IV of Scotland.

However, Henry VIII had removed Margaret and her descendants from the succession and so both claims failed.

(5) **Mary I** r.1553-1558 (half-sister of Edward VI)

Succeeded to the crown by:
M-PC, FC and SL (iii)

Although Mary was the eldest child and eventually succeeded to the throne, she did not, however, succeed because she *was* the eldest child; she succeeded because Henry VIII had made her and Elizabeth legitimate through the 1544 Act of Succession and because there was little support for Edward VI's "devise" for Lady Jane Grey to succeed him.

(6) **Elizabeth I** r.1558-1603 (half-sister of Mary I)

Succeeded to the crown by:
M-PC and SL (iii)

THE HOUSES OF STUART AND ORANGE
Family Trees 1603 – 1714

Mary Stuart Queen of Scots
b.1542 exec.1587
m. (ii) Lord Darnley
(see *Claim of Mary Queen of Scots*)

> **James I** of England **& VI** of Scotland
> [r.Scotland 1567-1603]
> [r.England & Scotland1603-1625]
> b.1564 d.1625
> m. Anne of Denmark

>> (1) Elizabeth
>> b.1596 d.1662
>> m. King Frederick of Bohemia d.1632

>>> Sophia
>>> b.1630 d.1714
>>> m. Earnest Augustus Elector of Hanover
>>> (Note 1)

>> (2) **Charles I**
>> [r.1625-1649] b.1600 exec.1649
>> m. Henrietta Maria

There were no monarchs during Cromwell's Commonwealth 1649-1660

> (i) **Charles II**
> [r.1660-1685] b.1630 d.1685
> m. Catherine of Braganza (Note 2)
>
> (ii) Mary Henrietta

b.1631 d.1660
m. William of Orange

William III (House of Orange)
[r.1689-1702] b.1650 d.1702 s.p.
m. Mary II (his first cousin**)

iii) **James II/VII**
[r.1685- dep.1688] b.1633 d.1701
m. (i) Anne Hyde d.1671 (Note 2)

(1) **Mary II**
[r.1689-1694] b.1662 d.1694 s.p.
m. **William III** (her first cousin**)

(2) **Anne**
[r.1702-1714]
b.1664/5 d.1714 s.p.
m. George of Denmark

Notes

1. Sophia pre-deceased Queen Anne by 2 months. We can only sympathize with Sophia who, had she lived another two months, would have been the last monarch from the House of Stuart…alas, it was not to be; that honour went to her first cousin once removed, Queen Anne. However, Sophia did posthumously become the mother of the first monarch from the House of Hanover.

2. Some members of Parliament became increasingly disturbed by James II/VII's leaning towards France and Catholicism. Things came to a head in 1688 when James' son, also called James, was born. It was clear that the new heir apparent would be brought up a Catholic. A group of Parliamentarians wanted James II/VII's daughter Mary, a

Protestant who was married to William of Orange, to succeed, and invited William to invade England, which he did in 1688. The bloodless invasion became known as the Glorious Revolution.

...how they got there
(For details of types of Primogeniture see Part 2)

(1) **James I/VI** r.1603-1625
   (1st cousin twice removed to Elizabeth I)

   Succeeded to the crown by: **M-PC, SL (iii)**

(2) **Charles I** r.1625-1648/49 (son of James I/VI)

   Succeeded to the crown by: **M-PC, SL (iii)**
   Other unsuccessful candidates:
   FC
   Elizabeth Stuart, Queen of Bohemia, (The Winter Queen), who was Charles I's elder sister, could legitimately have succeeded James I/VI under Full Cognatic primogeniture method. Elizabeth's grandson later became George I, the first Hanoverian King of England.

> **There were no monarchs during Cromwell's Commonwealth**
> **1649-1660 (The Interregnum)**

(3) **Charles II** r.1660-1684/85 d.s.p. (son of Charles I)

   Succeeded to the crown by: **M-PC, FC, SL (i)**

(4) **James II/VII** r.1684/85-1688
> (younger brother of Charles II)

> Succeeded to the crown by: **M-PC, SL (i)**

(5) **Mary II** r.1688-1694 jointly with her husband, William (see (6) below)
> (Mary was a daughter of James II/VII)

> Succeeded to the crown by: **FC, SL(iii)**
> > The birth of James II/VII's son, James Francis Edward (The Old Pretender), potentially changed the line of succession from Protestant back to Catholic. The new-born James was to be raised a Catholic and, therefore, like his father, was not acceptable as a King of England. On the other hand, the staunchly Protestant Mary Stuart (Mary II) was married to the equally staunchly Protestant William III of Orange – game over – with the blessing of the English Parliament, William invaded England in 1688 in a bloodless coup that became known as the "Glorious Revolution".

(6) **William III (of Orange)** singly r.1694-1702
> (nephew of James II/VII)

> Succeeded to the crown by: **FC**

(7) **Anne** r.1702-1714 d.s.p.s.
> (sister of Mary II and 1st cousin to William III)

> Succeeded to the crown by: **FC**

HOUSE OF HANOVER
Family Tree 1714 – 1901
(Offspring are inset below their parents)

From the House of Stuart:

Sophia (granddaughter of **James I/VI**)
b.1630 d.1714
m. Earnest Augustus, Elector of Hanover

George I
[r.1714-1727] b.1660 d.1727
m. Sophia Dorothea of Celle

George II
[r.1727-1760] b.1683 d.1760
m. Caroline of Ansbach

Frederick, Prince of Wales
b.1707 d.1751
m. Augusta of Saxe-Gotha

George III
[r.1760-1820]
b.1738 d.1820
m. Charlotte of Mecklenburg-Strelitz

(1 of 15) **George IV**
[r.1820-1830] b.1762 d.1830 s.p.m.s
m. Caroline of Brunswick

3) **William IV**
[r.1830-1837] b.1765 d.1837 d.s.p.s
m. Adelaide of Saxe-Meiningen

5) Prince Edward, Duke of Kent & Strathearn
b.1767 d.1820
m. Princess Victoria of Saxe-Coburg-Saalfeld

Victoria

> (daughter of Prince Edward, Duke off Kent & Strathearn)
> [r.1837-1901] b.1819 d.1901
> m. Prince Albert of Saxe-Coburg & Gotha b.1819 d.1861

...and how the Hanoverians got there

(For details of types of Primogeniture see Part 2)

(1) **George I** r.1714-1727 (3rd cousin to Anne)

Succeeded to the crown by:

The Act of Settlement (1701) prohibited Catholics from acceding to the throne of England. Over fifty Catholics were eliminated from the succession process before they found a Protestant in George Hanover.

(2) **George II** r.1727-1760 (son of George I)

Succeeded to the crown by:
M-PC, FC, SL (i)
Other unsuccessful candidates:
AS

George I's younger brother, Ernest Augustus, Duke of York and Albany, could legitimately have succeeded under the Agnatic Seniority method.

(3) **George III** r.1760-1820 (grandson of George II)

Succeeded to the crown by: **M-PC, SL (i)**
Other unsuccessful candidates:
FC

Princess Amelia, George II's eldest surviving child at the time of his death, could legitimately have succeeded.

AS

Prince William, Duke of Cumberland ("Butcher" Cumberland from the Battle of Culloden fame), a younger son of George II, could legitimately have succeeded under the Agnatic Seniority method.

(4) **George IV** r.1820-1830 d.s.p.s (son of George III)

Succeeded to the crown by: **M-PC, FC, SL (i)**

(5) **William IV** r.1830-1837 d.s.p.s
(younger brother of George IV)

Succeeded to the crown by:
M-PC, FC, SL (i), AS

(6) **Victoria** r.1837-1901 (niece of William IV)

Succeeded to the crown by: **M-PC, FC, SL (iii)**
Other unsuccessful candidates:

AS

Ernest Augustus I, King of Hanover, younger brother of Victoria's father, Prince Edward Duke of Kent and Strathearn, could legitimately have succeeded instead of Victoria under the little used, and therefore unsafe, Agnatic Seniority method. And there were four other brothers behind Ernest! – shades of Edward III.

HOUSE OF SAXE-COBURG & GOTHA
Family Tree 1901 – 1910
(Offspring are inset below their parents)

From the House of Hanover:

Victoria
[r.1837-1901] b.1819 d.1901
m. Prince Albert of Saxe-Coburg and Gotha
b.1819 d.1861

> (2 of 9) **Edward VII**
> [r.1901-1910]
> b.1841 d.1910
> m. Princess Alexandra of Denmark

...and how Edward got there
(For details of types of Primogeniture see Part 2)

(2) **Edward VII** r.1901-1910 (son of Victoria)

> Succeeded to the crown by: **M-PC, FC, SL (iii)**
> Other unsuccessful candidates:
> **AS**
>> The Princess Royal, Victoria, eldest child of Queen Victoria, could legitimately have succeeded instead of Edward VII. She died only nine months after Queen Victoria and would then have been succeeded by her eldest child, Kaiser Wilhelm II (just in case you were wondering what really started World War I).

HOUSE OF WINDSOR
Family Tree 1910 – current
(Offspring are inset below their parents)

On 17th July 1917, a royal proclamation changed the family surname from Saxe-Coburg and Gotha, to Windsor. Technically, therefore, the first seven years of George V's reign were under the banner of the House of Saxe-Coburg & Gotha.

George V (son of Edward VII)
[r.1910-1936] b.1865 d.1936
m. Princess Mary of Teck

> (1) **Edward VIII** (elder son of George V)
> [r.Jan1936 - abdicated11 Dec 1936]
> b.1894 d.1972 s.p.
> m. Wallis Simpson
>
> (2) **George VI**
> [r.1936-1952] b.1895 d.1952
> m. Elizabeth Bowes-Lyon
>
>> **Elizabeth II** (elder daughter of George VI)
>> [r.1952-   ] b.1926-
>> m.1947 Prince Philip (Mountbatten) of Greece
>> and Denmark, 1st Duke of Edinburgh
>> b.1921-

...and how the Windsors got there
(For details of types of Primogeniture see Part 2)

(1) **George V** r.1910-1936 (son of Edward VII)

Succeeded to the crown by: **M-PC, FC, SL (i)**

(2) **Edward VIII** r.1936 (not crowned) (son of George V)

> Succeeded to the crown by: **M-PC, FC, SL (i)**
> Edward VIII abdicated so that he could marry
> Wallis Simpson, a divorced woman.

(3) **George VI** r.1936-1952

> Succeeded to the crown by: **M-PC, SL (i)**

(4) **Elizabeth II** r.1952 – current 2018

> Succeeded to the crown by: **FC**
> Other unsuccessful candidates:
> **M-PC, AS**
>> Prince Henry, Duke of Gloucester (b. 31 March
>> 1900 d. 14 June 1974), the third son of George V,
>> could legitimately have succeeded instead of
>> Elizabeth II under both the Male-preference
>> Cognatic method (M-PC) and the Agnatic Seniority
>> method (AS).
> **SL (ii)**
>> Charles Prince of Wales (b. 14 November 1948)
>> could legitimately have succeeded instead of
>> Elizabeth II under the Semi-Salic Law (ii) method,
>> which permits the sons of women to inherit but not
>> women themselves. However, this method has
>> never been used in isolation in England.

PART 4

THE DOWNFALL OF THE PLANTAGENETS

The Plantagenets only had themselves to blame for losing their 330-year grip on the English crown – or 269 years if you accept that the House of Plantagenet only started with Henry III. The variety of primogeniture methods available to select an heir to the throne, combined with the fact that Edward III had five sons, made a family struggle for power inevitable. This surfeit of sons resulted in a thirty-year war, the 'Cousins' War', now commonly known as…

The War of the Roses

The Belligerents

> The House of Lancaster (Red Rose) represented by Henry VI and his Queen consort, Margaret of Anjou.
>
> *Versus*
>
> The House of York (White Rose) represented by Richard, 3rd Duke of York (Richard of York)

Shown below are the principal battles and adversaries during this thirty-year conflict.

THE BATTLES

1455 – 22 May
> **First Battle of St Albans** (Hertfordshire)
>> York:
>>> Richard of York;
>>> Richard Neville, Earl of Salisbury;
>>> Richard, 16th Earl of Warwick who was Salisbury's son and later became known as 'The Kingmaker'.
>> Lancaster:
>>> Henry VI (taken prisoner);

Edmund Beaufort, 2nd Duke of Somerset (k.i.b);
Humphrey Stafford, 1st Duke of Buckingham (taken
prisoner)

Victor:

House of York.

Outcome:

Richard of York was appointed Lord Protector.

1459 – 23 September
Battle of Blore Heath (Staffordshire)

York:

Richard Neville, Earl of Salisbury.

Lancaster:

James Tuchet, 5th Baron Audley (k.i.b)

Victor:

House of York.

Outcome:

The Lancastrians failed to prevent the Yorkist
forces at Middleham Castle in Yorkshire from
reaching the main Yorkist army at Ludlow Castle
in Shropshire.

1459 – 12 October
Battle of Ludford Bridge (Shropshire)

York:

Richard of York;
Richard Neville, Earl of Salisbury;
Richard, 16th Earl of Warwick (The Kingmaker)

Lancaster:

Henry VI;
Henry Stafford, 1st Duke of Buckingham.

Victor:

House of Lancaster – a rout.

Outcome:

York, Salisbury and Warwick were all attainted, however, the Lancastrian ascendancy was brief.

1460 – January
Battle of Sandwich (Kent)

York:

Richard Neville, 16th Earl of Warwick;
Edward Plantagenet, Earl of Cambridge (later Edward IV);
Sir John Denham.

Lancaster:

The King's sailors were still abed when Denham attacked.

Victor:

The House of York – a rout.

Outcome:

A minor sea skirmish off the coast of Sandwich that allowed Warwick and Cambridge to land in England on returning from Calais. They then headed north, via London, gathering forces as they went.

1460 – 10 July
Battle of Northampton

York:

Richard Neville, 16th Earl of Warwick;
Edward Plantagenet, Earl of Cambridge

Lancaster:

Henry VI (taken prisoner…again);
Humphrey Stafford, 1st Duke of Buckingham (k.i.b);
John Talbot, 2nd Earl of Shrewsbury (k.i.b)

Victor:

House of York – a rout.

Outcome:

A major battle in which the Yorkists were aided by the treacherous about face of Lord Grey of Ruthvin who switched his allegiance from Lancaster to York just as the battle commenced. The king was captured, but Warwick didn't know what to do with him – again.

1460 – 30 December
Battle of Wakefield (West Yorkshire)
York:

Richard of York (k.i.b);

Richard Neville, Earl of Salisbury (k.i.b)

Lancaster:

Henry Beaufort, 3rd Duke of Somerset; Henry Percy, Earl of Northumberland

Victor:

House of Lancaster

Outcome:

The victors killed many leaders of the Yorkist's cause, and then marched south.

1461 – 2 February
Battle of Mortimer's Cross (Herefordshire)
York:

Edward Plantagenet, Earl of Cambridge (became the 4th Duke of York following his father's death at Wakefield).

Lancaster:

Sir Owen Tudor (k.i.b). (Sir Owen was married to Catherine de Valois, widow of Henry V).

Victor:

House of York

Outcome:

The 18-year-old Edward Plantagenet's victory prevented Owen Tudor and his Welsh army from joining up with the main Lancastrian force.

1461 – 17 February

Second Battle of St Albans (Hertfordshire)

York:

Richard Neville, 16th Earl of Warwick.

Lancaster:

Margaret of Anjou, Queen consort to Henry VI.

Victor:

House of Lancaster

Outcome:

Warwick released Henry VI from captivity…again.

1461 – 28 March

Battle of Ferrybridge (Yorkshire)

York:

Richard Neville, 16th Earl of Warwick

Lancaster:

John Clifford, 9th Baron de Clifford (k.i.b)

Victor:

House of Lancaster

Outcome:

Lancastrians ambushed the Earl of Warwick who was wounded in the leg by an arrow, and his second-in-command was killed.

1461 – 29 March

Battle of Towton (Yorkshire)

York:

Edward, 4th Duke of York;

Richard Neville, 16th Earl of Warwick.

Lancaster:

Henry Beaufort, 3rd Duke of Somerset;

Henry Percy, Earl of Northumberland (k.i.b)

Victor:

House of York

Outcome:

The largest and one of the bloodiest battles ever fought on English soil, which resulted in Edward, 4th Duke of York, eventually claiming the crown as Edward IV.

1464 – 25 April

Battle of Hedgeley Moor (Northumberland)

York:

John Neville, 1st Marquess of Montagu.

Lancaster:

Henry Beaufort, 3rd Duke of Somerset.

Victor:

House of York

Outcome:

Enabled Parliament to negotiate a treaty with the Scots at York.

1464 – 15 May

Battle of Hexham (Yorkshire)

York:

John Neville, 1st Marquess of Montagu

Lancaster:

Henry Beaufort, 3rd Duke of Somerset (k.i.b)

Victor:

House of York

Outcome:

Lancastrians annihilated.

1469 – 26 July

Battle of Edgecote Moor (near Banbury, Oxfordshire)

York:

William Herbert, Earl of Pembroke (k.i.b).

Lancaster:

> Robin of Redesdale (real identity unknown) acting for Richard Neville, 16th Earl of Warwick. Warwick fell out with Edward IV because the latter had secretly married Elizabeth Woodville without telling him. This severely embarrassed Warwick who was negotiating a betrothal of Edward to a French princess when he learned of the king's marriage. Feeling increasingly marginalized by Edward IV, Warwick switched his allegiance to the Lancastrians.

Victor:

> House of Lancaster

Outcome:

> Led to Edward IV's brief capitulation.

1470 – 12 March

Battle of Losecoat Field

(near Empingham, Rutland. Losecoat, sometimes Losecote, means 'pigsty field')

York:

> Edward IV

Lancaster:

> Robert Welles, 8th Baron Willoughby de Eresby (k.i.b);
>
> Sir Robert Welles (son of the 8th Baron)

Victor:

> House of York

Outcome:

> Lord Willoughby de Eresby was beheaded in front of both armies. Warwick and George, Duke of Clarence (Edward IV's younger brother) who was married to a Neville, were implicated in the uprising and fled the country. The brothers later reconciled but not for long; George was executed in 1478.

1471 – 14 March

> **Battle of Ravenspur** (a former port at the mouth of the Humber near Hull)
>
>> This was not really a battle but merely the place where Edward IV landed to begin his mopping up operation.

1471 – 14 April

> **Battle of Barnet** (Hertfordshire)
>
>> York:
>>
>>> Edward IV; Richard, Duke of Gloucester (Edward's youngest brother who, through dubious means, later became Richard III).
>>
>> Lancaster:
>>
>>> Richard Neville, 16th Earl of Warwick (k.i.b); John Neville, 1st Marquess of Montagu (k.i.b);
>>> John de Vere, 13th Earl of Oxford
>>
>> Victor:
>>
>>> House of York
>>
>> Outcome:
>>
>>> A major battle and a decisive victory for the House of York that all but secured the throne for Edward IV.

1471 – 4 May

> **Battle of Tewkesbury** (Gloucestershire)
>
>> York:
>>
>>> Edward IV; Richard, Duke of Gloucester; William, 1st Baron Hastings
>>
>> Lancaster:
>>
>>> Edmund Beaufort, 4th Duke of Somerset (k.i.b);
>>> John Beaufort, Marquess of Dorset (k.i.b); John Courtney, Earl of Devon (k.i.b);

Edward, Prince of Wales (k.i.b) only son of Henry VI and Margaret of Anjou (taken prisoner).

Victor:

House of York

Outcome:

Major battle and a decisive victory for Edward IV.

A few days after the Battle of Tewkesbury, Henry VI died in the Tower of London under *mysterious circumstances*.

On Henry VI's death, the tried yet not always trusted method of male-preference cognatic primogeniture clearly identified Edward, eldest son of the late Richard of York, as Henry VI's heir presumptive. Edward was duly anointed as Edward IV. His eldest child, Elizabeth of York, later became queen consort to Henry VII...but not yet.

Up to this point, the war had been cousin against cousin; now it pitted brother against brother as the Plantagenet dynasty began to implode. George, Duke of Clarence, was executed in 1478 for plotting against his elder brother, Edward IV.

In Shakespeare's play, *The Life and Times of King Richard III*, George was drowned in a butt of Malmsey wine (a sweet, fortified Madeira wine originating in Greece) rather than beheaded, which was the more usual method of execution. And indeed, when George's body was exhumed years later, his head was still clearly attached to it. However, it is more likely that George's body was preserved in the butt (about 477 litres) of wine for the journey from the Tower of London to Tewkesbury Abbey, Gloucestershire, where he was buried. Therefore, the precise manner of George's execution remains yet another death surrounded by *mysterious circumstances*.

George initially turned against his elder brother because of the rumour that Edward IV was illegitimate and could not, therefore, legally inherit the crown. In fact, George could not prove that

Edward was illegitimate because all it took for a child to be accepted as legitimate in fifteenth century England was for the father to say "this is my child" – and it was – simple as that, no argument, all legal and above board. And that was precisely what Edward IV's father, Richard Plantagenet, 3rd Duke of York, had done. Edward IV was, therefore, legitimate according to the customs of the time and his ambitious younger brothers, George and Richard, could do nothing about it…

…or could they?

With the benefit of hindsight, perhaps killing his brother, George, was not such a smart move by Edward because it made their obnoxious and even more ambitious younger brother, Richard, Duke of Gloucester, the next in line – ignoring Edward's children, that is – but they were not a major problem for Richard.

And then, on 9th April 1483, a few days short of his 41st birthday, Edward IV died unexpectedly, and the Plantagenet dynasty finally began to unravel. The precise cause of Edward's death was never established – but there were rumours and again…*mysterious circumstances.*

Shakespeare, in *The Life and Times of King Richard III,* portrayed Edward's younger brother, the eponymous Richard, as the arch villain behind the King's death. And Shakespeare was probably right.

Nevertheless, as far as the succession was concerned, Edward IV's death should not have been a problem. After all, he had two sons, also called Edward and Richard just to confuse matters, and a daughter, Elizabeth, who was later to play such an important role in the creation of the House of Tudor.

The malevolent and ambitious Richard, upon hearing of his brother's death, which presumably came as no great surprise to him, immediately tossed his two young nephews in the Tower of London – for their own safety, of course. Even so, there was no doubting the *mysterious circumstances* of their complete disappearance. Richard didn't bother with the girl – big mistake! As for the boys, alas, they were never seen again, and Richard quickly claimed the throne to become Richard III.

Yet enough was enough; the country was tired of being torn apart by war, and so the stage was set for Henry Tudor's entry into history.

However, there was one more Plantagenet king to eliminate: Richard III, (well, two if you count the infant Edward V, but he was already in the Tower and was never seen again) and at least one more battle to fight:

Sometime, c.1430, well before the Cousins' War started, Henry V's widow, Catherine de Valois, had married Owen Tudor. They had a son, Edmund, who was therefore Henry VI's half-brother. This relationship was not lost on Edmund's eventual wife, the ambitious Lady Margaret Beaufort.

The Beaufort name is a giveaway here: it signifies a bastard line from John of Gaunt and his mistress, Katherine Swynford. The line was later legitimised but with the normal proviso for bastard lines that no Beaufort could ever succeed to the throne. And three Beauforts – the 2nd, 3rd and 4th Dukes of Somerset – were all descended from John of Gaunt, all related to Lady Margaret, and all killed during, or just after, different battles during the War of the Roses. Like the Dukes of Somerset, Lady Margaret was, therefore, a Plantagenet directly descended from Edward III. However, by her marriage to Edmund Tudor, she was to become the mother of the first Tudor monarch of England: Henry VII…

1485 – 22 August
The Battle of Bosworth Field…

Under an overcast sky on a marshy field in the heart of Leicestershire, the armies of Henry Tudor, Earl of Richmond, and the Plantagenet king, Richard III, prepared to do battle.

Out-numbered two-to-one by Richard's forces – some historians dispute this ratio – things did not look too good for Henry. But Richard also had a problem: he knew that the powerful Lord Thomas Stanley, despite pledging his allegiance to Richard, could not be relied upon because, three years earlier in 1482, Stanley had married Henry Tudor's widowed mother, the ambitious Lady Margaret Beaufort. Stanley was, therefore, Henry Tudor's stepfather.

Would Stanley support his stepson or the king?

Both Henry and Richard were only too well aware that Stanley's large force together with that of his brother, Sir William Stanley, would be crucial to the outcome of the battle.

So, the astutely malevolent Richard took precautions: he grabbed Thomas Stanley's son, George, and threatened to kill him, if the Stanley brothers changed sides. Allegedly, Lord Stanley simply replied: "Your Majesty forgets that I have other sons," or words to that effect. One wonders what George felt about that.

The Stanley brothers held their forces to either side of the marshy field and watched as the slightly deformed, ambitious, and possibly psychotic, Richard III charged his army straight at Henry Tudor.

Seeing that Henry was under severe pressure, Sir William Stanley intervened. His troops quickly surrounded Henry to protect him from Richard's advancing forces. The king was furious at Stanley's betrayal. Unseated *('A horse, a horse, my kingdom for a horse')* and wild beyond reason, Richard plunged into the fray intent on personally killing Henry. He didn't make it; a mighty blow from one of Sir William's men split open Richard's skull, killing him instantly.

After that, the fierce battle was soon over. With more than a little help from the Stanley brothers, Henry Tudor had wrested the crown from Richard III.

As for Richard, he was taken from the field and buried in a Franciscan Friary in Leicester. Years later, sometime between 1536 and 1539, Henry VIII destroyed the Friary during his Dissolution of the Monasteries and all trace of Richard was lost – until 2012! That year, a team of archaeologists excavating a car park in Leicester discovered what they believed to be Richard's remains. This was later confirmed by DNA tests. He was not too difficult to identify because Richard, like Robert Cecil, suffered from scoliosis (curvature of the spine). In Richard's case, one shoulder appeared slightly higher than the other, whereas Robert Cecil had a far more pronounced hunched back.

> 'I, that am rudely stamp'd, and want love's
> majesty
> To strut before a wanton ambling nymph;
> I, that am curtail'd of this fair proportion,
> Cheated of feature by dissembling nature,
> Deform'd, unfinish'd, sent before my time
> Into this breathing world, scarce half made up,

And that so lamely and unfashionable
That dogs bark at me as I halt by them.'

It is Richard III speaking in the play, of course, but why did Shakespeare depict him in a manner that better described Robert Cecil? What possible motive could a country lad from Warwickshire have for doing that? The speech reads more as if the author wants to make it perfectly clear that he was not a Plantagenet supporter and never had been. William Shakespeare had no reason to do that, yet there were many at Court who did...but that's another story.

Oh, and you will be pleased to know that George Stanley, also known as Lord Strange, survived despite his father's callous remark to Richard III before Bosworth. In fact, George's father who, you may recall, was Henry VII's stepfather, was created the 1st Earl of Derby in October 1485. No surprise there.

Thus, the Plantagenet years ended; the door finally closed on England's Mediaeval Period; and Modern History dawned with a new king, a new dynasty and new problems – *Enter Henry VII and the House of Tudor.*

PART 5

THE RISE AND FALL OF THE HOUSE OF TUDOR

As a family, the Tudors were misfits; they were too much to one side, far too lineally challenged, to inherit the throne. Yet inherit it they did, and the country was, internally at least, relatively peaceful during most of the Tudor years. Unlike the Plantagenets, the eventual Tudor discords occurred through religion rather than kinship. And the discords started in earnest after the death of the third Tudor king, the young Protestant Edward VI, with the natural succession of his elder half-sister, the Catholic Mary I.

THE PRETENDERS
THE CLAIM OF LADY JANE DUDLEY (NÉE GREY)
(A Protestant Claimant)

Of course, Lady Jane Grey was not the only person with a claim to the throne – even her mother had a better claim than she did. However, her mother, Frances Brandon, obviously wasn't interested in the plotting of John Dudley, the self-styled Duke of Northumberland, as witnessed by the fact that she remarried in indecent haste only months after her first husband's execution.

The duchess's new husband was Adrian Stokes who was her Master of the Horse and, if that wasn't bad enough, a commoner – Oh dear!

LADY JANE GREY – Family Tree

Henry VII
[r.1485-1509] b.1457 d.1509
m.1486 Elizabeth of York
d.1503

4) Mary Tudor
b.1495/6 d.1533
m. (i) 1514 Louis XII King of France b.1462 d.1514/15
s.p.
m. (ii) Charles Brandon, 1st Duke of Suffolk
b.1484 d.1545
Charles and Mary married secretly in France on 5th
March1514/5 and officially at Greenwich Palace on 13th
May 1515.

> (i) Frances Brandon
> b.1517 d.1559
> m. (ii)1555 Adrian Stokes b.1519 d.1586 s.p.s.
> m. (i)1534 Henry Grey, 1st Duke of Suffolk,
> Marquess of Dorset
> b.1517 exec.1555
>
>> (1) **Jane** Grey
>> [r. for 9 days] b.1537 exec.1554 s.p.
>> m.1553 Guildford Dudley brother of Robert
>> Dudley, Earl of Leicester.
>>
>> (2) Catherine Grey
>> b.1538 d.1568
>> m.(i)1553 (annulled 1554) Henry Herbert
>> m. (ii) 1560 (secretly) Edward Seymour,
>> Earl of Hertford (issue not shown)
>
> (ii) Eleanor Brandon
> b.1519 d.1547
> m. 1533 Henry Clifford, 2nd Earl of Cumberland
> b.1517 d.1569

THE CLAIMS OF MARY QUEEN OF SCOTS
and ARABELLA STUART

Life started well enough for Mary – just look at her CV: daughter of King James V of Scotland; grand-niece and possible heir to Henry VIII of England; Queen of Scotland at only six days (yes, days!) old; and engaged to the dauphin of France when she was but a wee lass of five. With that CV, you would be forgiven for thinking that Mary Stuart (she favoured the French spelling of Stewart) was set for a rosy future overflowing with power and privilege.

Sadly, it was not to be.

Mary was fifteen when she eventually married the dauphin who was nearly two years her junior. The year after her marriage, 1559, her father-in-law, Henry II of France, died. Mary's stammering young husband was now King Francis II of France and she, his Queen consort.

All right so far!

Unfortunately, the following year, 1560, was a bad year for young Mary Stuart: in June, her mother, Mary of Guise, died. She had been running Scotland, with the aid of the French, on behalf of her daughter who was still a minor. Tragedy struck again only six months later, when Mary Stuart's sickly young husband also died.

Thus, within six months and only days after her eighteenth birthday, Mary had become both an orphan and a widow. Grief stricken, she returned to Scotland where, in August 1561, she landed at the Edinburgh port of Leith on the south bank of the Firth of Forth. Although greeted with rapture by the Scottish people, she was too Catholic for the Protestant lords of

Scotland; too fun loving for the dour Presbyterians; too tall for the men at Court - she was five feet eleven inches (180 centimetres) tall; and far too young, intelligent and sophisticated in general. Yet her subjects loved her.

And then the English got involved in Mary's life. Queen Elizabeth I of England put forward her favourite, Robert Dudley, soon to be created the 1st Earl of Leicester, as a suitable candidate for Mary's next husband. Perhaps Elizabeth liked the idea of a child fathered by Leicester succeeding her as Queen of England and Scotland, even if that child were not of her own loins. Leicester, however, didn't like the idea at all and soon found an ally in the Queen's chief minister, Sir William Cecil, later the 1st Baron Burghley.

The canny Cecil had a better idea for a suitor: Henry Stewart (he favoured the Scottish spelling), Lord Darnley.

Darnley was three years younger than Mary, and he was her first cousin. As both were grandchildren of Margaret Tudor, Henry VIII's elder sister, any issue from a marriage between them (as James I/VI eventually was) would have Tudor blood in its veins from both parents. No doubt this symmetry of lineage appealed to Cecil. Surprisingly, it did not appeal to Elizabeth who thought that such a union would be a threat to her crown and her life.

Elizabeth's objections notwithstanding, Mary and Darnley were married on Monday, 9th July 1565, in the Chapel-Royal of Holyrood Palace, (or the Palace of Holyroodhouse) Edinburgh. Their son, James Stuart, was born on 19th June 1566.

Queen Elizabeth was furious at the union. She believed that Darnley, being an English subject and the son of an earl, should have obtained her consent before marrying anyone; he failed to do so. For her part, Mary, being a Catholic, should have obtained a dispensation from the Pope before marrying her first cousin, even though Darnley was from a Catholic family; there is no record that she did so.

Darnley proved to be an immature, jealous, egotistical, syphilitic bully who wanted to rule Scotland in his own right. Furthermore, he convinced himself that James was not his child but the product of an affair between Mary and her Italian secretary, David Rizzio (or Riccio). It has been suggested that Darnley also had a sexual relationship with Rizzio, which then raises the question: was he jealous of Mary or David? Either way, on 9th March 1566 Darnley had Rizzio brutally murdered in front of Mary.

On 10th February 1567, less than a year after the bloody murder of Rizzio, Lord Darnley was found strangled at Kirk O'Field not ten minutes from Holyrood.

Enter James Hepburn, 4th Earl of Bothwell.

Well, that is not strictly true because Mary and Bothwell were already well acquainted. In fact, in 1560, when Mary was the seventeen-year-old Queen of France, she had given Bothwell 600 crowns, a position at the French Court and the income of a gentleman. And in February 1566, she attended his marriage to the wealthy Lady Jean Gordon, daughter of the 4th Earl of Huntly.

And then, one year after his wedding, Bothwell was charged with the murder of Darnley. The trial lasted less than a day, and Bothwell was acquitted. The main reason for the quick acquittal was that the principal witness for the prosecution, Darnley's father, the Earl of Lennox, failed to appear. Not surprising really, because he was on his way to the court accompanied by his

3,000 supporters, when Bothwell's 4,000 supporters intercepted him. No contest. Justice would have to wait – but it did not have to wait very long.

Mary married Bothwell in a Protestant wedding ceremony at Holyrood Palace on 15th May 1567, only eight days after he divorced Lady Jean. The marriage divided the nation. Within a month, the country had had enough of them. Mary was imprisoned in Loch Leven Castle, while Bothwell fled to Norway and on to Denmark. They never met again.

Mary Stuart was destined to spend the rest of her life under house arrest in various stately homes in England until her execution on 8th February 1587; Bothwell, on the other hand, went mad in Denmark's infamous Dragsholme Castle where he died in 1578.

By the summer of 1587, Mary Queen of Scots had been executed, while her son, James, was still unmarried. Thus, at that time, the English born Protestant, Arabella Stuart, granddaughter of the notorious Bess of Hardwick, Countess of Shrewsbury, was second in line to the thrones of both Scotland and England – see family trees below.

THE CLAIM OF MARY QUEEN OF SCOTS

Henry VII
(See Tudor Family Tree for details of other offspring)

2) Margaret Tudor
b.1489 d.1541
m. (i) 1503 **James IV** of Scotland [r.1488-1513]
b.1473 d.1513

James V of Scotland [r.1513-1542] b.1512 d.1542
m. (i) 1537 Madeliene de Valois d.1537 s.p.
m. (ii) 1538 Marie of Guise b.1515 d.1560

Mary (Mary Stuart, Queen of Scots)
[r.1542-1567] b.1542 exec.1587
m. (i) 1558 Francois II of France b.1544 d.1560
s.p.
m. (iii) 1567 James Hepburn, 4th Earl of Bothwell
b.c. 1534 d.1578 s.p.
m. (ii) 1565 Henry Stuart, Lord Darnley (her 1st
cousin)

James I/VI
King of Scotland [r.1567-1625]
King of England, Scotland and Ireland
[r.1603-1625] b.1567 d.1625
m. 1589 Ann of Denmark
b.1574 d.1619 (issue – see family tree for
the *Houses of Stuart and Orange*)

THE CLAIM OF ARABELLA STUART

Henry VII
(See Tudor Family Tree for details of other offspring)

2) Margaret Tudor
b.1489 d.1541
m. (i) 1503 **James IV** of Scotland [r.1488-1513]
b.1473 d.1513
m. (ii) 1514 (div. 1527) Archibald Douglas, 6th Earl of Angus
b.1489 d.1557

Margaret Douglas
b.1515 d.1578
m. 1544 Matthew Stuart, 4th Earl of Lennox
b.1516 d.1571

(1) Henry Stuart, Lord Darnley b.1545 d.1567
m. 1565 Mary Stuart, Queen of Scots (1st cousin)
(See *Claim of Mary Stuart* for issue)

(2) Charles Stuart b.1556 d.1576
m.c.1574 Elizabeth Cavendish

Arabella (Arbella) Stuart
b.1575 d.1615 (died in the Tower of London)
m.1610 (secretly) William Seymour, 2nd Duke of Somerset b.1588 d.1660 s.p.

Meanwhile, the Spanish were preparing to invade…yet there was one more, albeit not very ambitious, pretender…

CLAIM OF HENRY HASTINGS
3rd EARL OF HUNTINGDON

Edward III	
(see House of Plantagenet (2))	
(2) Lionel of Antwerp, 1st Duke of Clarence d.1368	(4) Edmund of Langley, 1st Duke of York d.1402
Philippa Mortimer	Richard, 3rd Earl of Cambridge m. Anne Mortimer, niece of Elizabeth*
Elizabeth* Mortimer	Richard Plantagenet, 3rd Duke of York m. Cecily Neville, a granddaughter of John of Gaunt.
Henry Percy, 2nd Earl of Northumberland	George Plantagenet, 1st Duke of Clarence. George was the younger brother of Edward IV and the elder brother of Richard III.
Henry Percy, 3rd Earl of Northumberland	Margaret Plantagenet exec.1541 (Beatified 1886)
Anne Percy	Henry de la Pole, 1st Baron Montague exec.1539
Mary 4th Baroness Hungerford	**Catherine de la Pole m. 1532 Francis Hastings**

64

George Hastings, 1st Earl of Huntingdon	
Francis Hastings, 2nd Earl of Huntingdon m. 1532 Catherine de la Pole	

Henry Hasting was descended from Edward III on both sides of his family tree, as shown above. Despite this rather tenuous claim, it explains why the Tudors were paranoid about him. Little wonder that at least eight of his antecedents were either executed or died in battle. However, in fairness to the Tudors, only three of those deaths occurred after 1485.

Francis Hastings and Catherine de la Pole were sixth cousins twice removed.

THE TUDOR RELATIVES and FAVOURITES

THE HOWARD and BOLEYN CONNECTIONS

Thomas Howard, 2nd Duke of Norfolk
b.1443 d.1524
m. (i) 1472 Elizabeth Tilney d.1497

> (1) Edmund Howard b.c.1478 d.1539
> m.(i) Joyce Culpeper d.1531
>
> > Catherine Howard b.c.1521 exec.1542
> > m. 1540 **Henry VIII** (5th wife)
>
> (2) Elizabeth Howard b.c.1480 d.1538
> m.c.1498 Thomas Boleyn,
> 1st Earl of Wiltshire & Ormonde d.1539
>
> > Anne Boleyn, Marquess of Pembroke b.c.1501
> > exec.1536
> > m. 1533 **Henry VIII** (2nd wife)
> >
> > > **Elizabeth I**
> > > [r.1558 – 1603] b.1533 d.1603 (Never
> > > married)

THE HOWARD, DE VERE and STANLEY CONNECTIONS

Thomas Howard, 2nd Duke of Norfolk b.1443 d.1524
m. (ii) 1497 Agnes Tilney d.1545
Agnes was cousin to Thomas's first wife, Elizabeth – see the
Howard and Boleyn connections above.

(1) Anne Howard
m. John de Vere, 14th Earl of Oxford b.1457 d.1526

John de Vere, 15th Earl of Oxford b.1482 d.1540
m. (ii) Elizabeth Trussell b.1496 d.1527

John de Vere, 16th Earl of Oxford b.1516 d.1562
m. (ii) Margery Golding

Edward de Vere, 17th Earl of Oxford b.1550
d.1604
m.(ii) 1589 Elizabeth Trentham b.c.1562
d.c.1612
m.(i) 1571 Anne Cecil b.1556 d.1588

Elizabeth de Vere b.1575 d.1627
m.1595 William Stanley, 6th Earl of
Derby (her 2nd cousin twice removed)

(2) Dorothy Howard
m. Edward Stanley, 3rd Earl of Derby b.1509 d.1572

Henry Stanley, 4th Earl of Derby b.1531 d.1593
m.1555 Margaret Clifford (granddaughter of Mary
Tudor sister of **Henry VIII**)

William Stanley, 6th Earl of Derby (Note 1)
b.c.1561 d.1642
(William succeeded his brother, Ferdinando
Stanley, 5th Earl of Derby b.c.1559 d.1594)

m.1595 Elizabeth de Vere (daughter of the 17th Earl of Oxford and Anne Cecil – see above)

(3) William Howard, 1st Baron Howard of Effingham
b.1510 d.1572/3
m. Margaret Gamage b.unkn d.1581

> Charles Howard, 1st Earl of Nottingham Lord High Admiral b.1536 d.1596
> m.(i) 1563 Catherine Carey
> (daughter of Lord Hunsdon) (Issue: 5)
> m.(ii) 1603 Margaret Stuart b.c.1590 d.1639 (Issue: 2)

Notice how the families are united by marriage. The de Veres fought for the Lancastrians during the War of the Roses, while the Stanleys famously switched sides at Bosworth Field to allow the Tudor victory. Here both families became united under the Howard Catholic banner.

HASTINGS, BOLEYN, LEICESTER and ESSEX CONNECTIONS

George Hastings, 1st Earl of Huntingdon b.1488 d.1544
m.1509 Anne Stafford b.c.1483 d.1544

Anne Stafford was the widow of William Herbert, 1st Earl of Pembroke, and the daughter of Henry Stafford, 2nd Duke of Buckingham. She was allegedly a mistress of Henry VIII.

> Dorothy b.c.1516 d.after 1562
> m.c. 1536 Sir Richard Devereux b.c.1504 d.1547

> > **Walter Devereux, 1st Earl of Essex** b.c.1539
> > d.1576 (suddenly)
> > m. 1562 Lettice Knollys (see below)

> > > Robert Devereux 2nd Earl of Essex
> > > b.1566 exec.1600/1
> > > m. 1590 (secretly) Frances Walsingham
> > >
> > > Frances was the widow of Sir Philip Sidney and daughter of Sir Francis Walsingham.

Thomas Boleyn, Earl of Wiltshire & Ormonde b.c.1477 d.1539
m.c.1498 Elizabeth Howard b.c.1480 d.1538

Elizabeth was a daughter of the 2nd Duke of Norfolk, while Thomas Boleyn was the maternal grandfather of Queen Elizabeth I.

> (1) Mary Boleyn b.c.1499 d.1543
> m. (ii) c.1534 Sir William Stafford
> m. (i)1520 William Carey b.c.1500 d.1528

Mary Boleyn was allegedly the mistress of both Henry VIII and King Francis I of France. Did Queen Elizabeth know, or at least suspect, that Lettice Knollys was her half-great niece and that Elizabeth's favourite, Robert Devereux, Earl of Essex, might therefore have had misguided ideas of obtaining the crown himself notwithstanding that, if true, he came from a distant and illegitimate line?

(i) Henry Carey, 1st Baron Hunsdon b.1526 d.1596
m.1545 Anne Morgan b.c.1529 d.1607 (Issue not shown)

Catherine, one of Lord Hunsdon's 12 children, (not to be confused with Catherine Carey, his sister, below) married Charles Howard 1st Earl of Nottingham.

(ii) Catherine Carey b.c.1524 d.1569
m. 1540 Sir Francis Knollys b.c.1514 d.1596

Lettice Knollys b.1543 d.1634
m.(i) 1562 Walter Devereux
m.(ii) 1578 Robert Dudley,1st Earl of Leicester b.c.1532 d.1588
m.(iii) 1589 Sir Christopher Blount b.c.1556 exec.1601

Only six months after the death of her second husband, Robert Dudley, Earl of Leicester, Lettice married Sir Christopher Blount, a much younger man and head of Robert Dudley's household ...Oh dear, little wonder that Queen Elizabeth called Lettice a 'she wolf'.

(2) Anne Boleyn b.c.1501 exec.1536
m. 1533 **Henry VIII**

> **Elizabeth I**
> (see *House of Tudor* for details)

(3) George Boleyn, Viscount Rochford b.c.1503
exec.1536
m.c. 1525 Jane Parker b.c.1505 exec.1542 (No known issue)

Jane Parker was executed with Catherine Howard.

PART 6

THE ENGLISH CIVIL WARS 1642-1651

The English Civil Wars were a direct result of Charles I's disagreement with Parliament over three of the fundamental elements of government at the time: power, money and religion.

Power: Charles I, like his father, James I/IV, before him, believed in the divine right of kings to rule, and he wanted to control both the army and Parliament.

Money: Charles I only required Parliament to meet when he needed it to raise money for him.

Religion: Charles I's wife, Henrietta Maria, was a Catholic and not trusted, while the Puritans feared that the king's High Anglican leanings were getting too close to Catholicism for comfort.

No Parliament: 1629 – 1640

Personal rule of Charles I – his attempt to raise taxes without Parliament's approval caused considerable unease throughout the land. Charles effectively became a dictator.

The Short Parliament: 1640 (three weeks 13 April to 3 May)

The king asked Parliament to raise funds for his struggle with Scotland in the Bishops' War (1639–1640). That war was Scotland's response to Charles I's requirement for episcopacy (a Church ruled by bishops) whereas the Scots favoured a Presbyterian system (without bishops). The Parliament was a fiasco.

The Long Parliament: 1640–1660

On 4 January 1642, the king, acting on rumours that his wife, Queen Henrietta Maria, was about to be impeached by the Dissenters (Puritans) for her alleged involvement in Catholic plots, marched into the House of Commons with an armed guard. He was determined to arrest the Five Members (as they became known) of Parliament that he held primarily responsible for this outrage and have them tried for treason. He was too late; they had been tipped off and were not in the House. The Speaker of the House of Commons, William Lenthall, to his everlasting credit, declined to tell the king where they were. Fearing for his life, Charles I fled with his family and supporters to Oxford.

The Five Members:

John Hampden (c.b.1595 d.1643)
Arthur Haselrig (b.1601 d.1661)
Denzil Holles (b.1599 d.1680)
John Pym (b.1584 d.1643)
William Strode (b.1598 d.1645)
There was also one Dissenter from the House of Lords: Edward Montagu, Viscount Mandeville (later 2nd Earl of Manchester) (b.1602 d.1671)

With the king setting up a Royalist Parliament in Oxford, civil war became inevitable.

The Belligerents

The Royalists; supporters of Charles I who were also known as Caveliers.
Versus

The Parliamentarians; also known as Puritans or Roundheads and were eventually represented by Oliver Cromwell.

BATTLES OF THE FIRST CIVIL WAR

1642 – 23 October

Battle of Edgehill (Warwickshire)

Royalists:

Charles I;

Prince Rupert of the Rhine who was married to Elizabeth Stuart, daughter of James I/VI and sister of Charles I.

Parliamentarians:

Robert Devereux, 3rd Earl of Essex

Victor:

Indecisive

Outcome:

Essex withdrew to Warwick leaving the road to London open for Charles.

1642 – 12 November

Battle of Brentford (Middlesex)

Royalists:

Prince Rupert of the Rhine.

Parliamentarians:

Captain John Lilburne. (Over a century later, Lilburne's stubborn agitation for 'freeborn rights' became the catalyst for the 5th Amendment to the United States of America's constitution).

Victor:

Royalists.

Outcome:

The Royalists unwisely sacked the town thereby converting many Londoners to the Parliamentarians cause.

1643 – 30 June

> **Battle of Adwalton Moor** (Yorkshire)
>
> Royalists:
>
> > William Cavendish, Earl of Newcastle-upon-Tyne (later 1st Duke of Newcastle)
>
> Parliamentarians:
>
> > Sir Thomas Fairfax;
> >
> > Major General Gifford.
>
> Victor:
>
> > Royalists who outnumbered the opposition by nearly three-to-one.
>
> Outcome:
>
> > Consolidated the Royalist position in the north.

1643 – 4 July

> **Battle of Burton Bridge** (Staffordshire)
>
> Royalists:
>
> > Queen Henrietta Maria, the unpopular Catholic wife of Charles I;
> >
> > Thomas Tyldesley (knighted after the battle)
>
> Parliamentarians:
>
> > Richard Houghton (taken prisoner);
> >
> > Thomas Sanders (taken prisoner)
>
> Victor:
>
> > Royalists
>
> Outcome:
>
> > Allowed Henrietta Maria to deliver arms to Charles I's army.

1643 – 5 July

> **Battle of Lansdowne** (near Bath, Somerset)
>
> Royalists:
>
> > Sir Ralph Hopton, later 1st Baron Hopton (wounded);
> >
> > Sir Bevil Grenville (k.i.b)

Parliamentarians:

Sir William Waller

Victor:

Indecisive

Outcome:

Little was achieved by either side.

1643 – 13 July

Battle of Roundway Down (near Devizes, Wiltshire)

Royalists:

Ralph, Lord Hopton;

Henry, Lord Wilmot (1st Earl of Rochester from 1652)

Parliamentarians:

Sir William Waller

Victor:

Royalists – decisive victory

Outcome:

Led by Lord Wilmot, this was reputedly the greatest cavalry victory of the English Civil War. The West Country, and the port of Bristol in particular, was now firmly under Royalist control.

1643 – 20 September

First Battle of Newbury (Berkshire)

Royalists:

Charles I;

Prince Rupert of the Rhine;

Sir John Byron

Parliamentarians:

Robert Devereux, 3rd Earl of Essex;

Sir Philip Stapleton

Victor:

Parliamentarians – decisive victory

Outcome:

This victory turned the tide against the Royalists, and Essex received a hero's welcome in London.

1643 – 11 October

    Winceby (Near Horncastle, Lincolnshire)

    Royalists:

        Sir William Widdrington

    Parliamentarians:

        Oliver Cromwell

        Sir Thomas Fairfax (Black Tom)

    Victor:

        Parliamentarians – decisive victory

    Outcome:

        This minor battle turned into a bloody massacre of the local villagers by Cromwell. It was the first time that he had fought alongside Thomas Fairfax. Later, they would control the New Model Army.

1644 – 29 June

    Battle of Cropredy Bridge (near Banbury, Oxfordshire)

    Royalists:

        Charles I

    Parliamentarians:

        Sir William Waller

    Victor:

        Royalists

    Outcome:

        Waller's army was demoralized and many deserted. Charles I safely ignored him after the battle and headed west to confront the Earl of Essex at Lostwithiel.

1644 – 2 July

    Battle of Marston Moor (North Yorkshire)

    Royalists:

        Prince Rupert of the Rhine:

        William Cavendish, Marquess of Newcastle

Parliamentarians:
>> Edward Montagu, 2nd Earl of Manchester
>> Ferdinando Fairfax, 2nd Lord Fairfax of Cameron
>> Earl of Leven (Scottish Covenanters)
>> Oliver Cromwell

Victor:
>> Parliamentarians

Outcome:
>> A decisive victory in which Cromwell's cavalry was significant. The Parliamentarians gained control of the North.

1644 – 2 September
Battle of Lostwithiel (Cornwall)
Royalists:
>> Charles I

Parliamentarians:
>> Robert Devereux, 3rd Earl of Essex

Victor:
>> Royalists.

Outcome:
>> This was the last major victory for the Royalists after which Charles I set off for London.

1644 – 27 October
Second Battle of Newbury (Berkshire)
Royalists:
>> Charles I
>> Prince Maurice, younger brother of Prince Rupert of the Rhine.

Parliamentarians:
>> Robert Devereux, 3rd Earl of Essex;
>> Edward Montagu, 2nd Earl of Manchester;
>> Sir William Wallace

Victor:
>> Indecisive

Outcome:

> Charles I was outnumbered and his return to London blocked; he retreated to Oxford.

1645 – 14 June

Battle of Naseby (Northamptonshire)

Royalists:

> Charles I
>
> Prince Rupert of the Rhine.

Parliamentarians:

> Sir Thomas Fairfax (Black Tom), eldest son of Ferdinando, 2nd Lord Fairfax of Cameron;
>
> Oliver Cromwell.

Victor:

> Parliamentarians

Outcome:

> Charles I's army was all but destroyed. His secret papers were captured, which confirmed that he was seeking external Catholic support for his cause.

BATTLES OF THE SECOND CIVIL WAR

1648 – 8 May

Battle of St Fagans (Wales)

Royalists:

Colonel John Poyers, Governor of Pembroke Castle

Parliamentarians:

Colonel Thomas Horton

Victor:

Parliamentarians

Outcome:

Horton, leading a detachment of the New Model Army, defeated a force of former Parliamentarians who rebelled because they had not been paid. Poyers retreated to Pembroke Castle, which was then besieged until it finally capitulated on 11 July after Cromwell's forces managed to cut off the water supply to the castle.

1648 – 1 June

Battle of Maidstone (Kent)

Royalists:

George Goring, 1st Earl of Norwich

Parliamentarians:

Sir Thomas Fairfax (Black Tom)

Victor:

Parliamentarians

Outcome:

Royalists retreated first to London and then to Colchester.

1648 – 17-19 August

Battle of Preston (Lancashire)

Royalists:

James Hamilton, 1st Duke of Hamilton

Parliamentarians:

Oliver Cromwell
John Lambert
Victor:
Parliamentarians
Outcome:
A decisive victory, which ended the second civil war.

THE RUMP PARLIAMENT

In September 1648, the Long Parliament became increasingly fearful of the power and radical ideas of the New Model Army and wanted to reinstate Charles I with the proviso that, under the proposed Treaty of Newport, the king's powers would be greatly restricted. In what was effectively a military coup, the New Model Army, then under the control of Thomas Fairfax, prevented 231 supporters of the treaty, of whom 45 were imprisoned, from voting in the House. The remaining members became known as the Rump Parliament and implemented the policy of the New Model Army with the result that in...

1649 – 30 January

Charles I was executed outside Banqueting House, Whitehall, London

1649 – 19 May

The Rump Parliament declared England a Commonwealth.

BATTLES OF THE THIRD CIVIL WAR

1650 – 3 September
Battle of Dunbar (East Lothian, Scotland)
Royalists:
David Leslie (later 1st Lord Newark)
Parliamentarians:
Oliver Cromwell
Victor:
Parliamentarians
Outcome:
The Scottish army was decimated allowing Cromwell to take Edinburgh and eventually Edinburgh Castle.

1651 – 3 September
Battle of Worcester (Worcestshire)
Royalists:
Charles II
Parliamentarians:
Oliver Cromwell
Victor:
Parliamentarians
Outcome:
A decisive victory that ended the English Civil Wars.

1653 – 16 December
Oliver Cromwell sworn in as Lord Protector for life.

1660 – 29 May
The Restoration of the monarchy: Charles II crowned on 23 April 1661.

THE LAST BATTLE ON BRITISH SOIL?

There are many contenders, but it really depends on what constitutes a 'battle'. Most definitions are similar and similarly vague. Note this from Funk and Wagnall (1981):

> A *battle* is a <u>more or less</u> continuous fight and <u>may</u> last for many days, while a *skirmish* is <u>brief </u>and involves <u>small groups</u> of combatants. An *action* is one of the events in a battle…

> A *siege* is the act of surrounding any fortified area with the intention of capturing it.

1685
On the early morning of 16 July (Gregorian), the last battle of the ill-fated Monmouth rebellion took place on Sedgemoor (about 3 miles (5 kilometres) southeast of Bridgwater, Somerset). Although short, this was a battle by any definition. The Duke of Monmouth's forces, estimated at 3,500, outnumbered the Royalists of King James II/VII led by the experienced Lord Feversham. However, the rebels were no match for the Royalist cavalry and the battle lasted only five hours. This is a valid contender for the last battle fought on *English* soil.

1688
Battle of Reading was the only serious conflict during the Glorious Revolution, and yet it was little more than a siege with the small force supporting William of Orange being victorious.

1715
The Battle of Preston fought during the First Jacobite Rising was also a siege rather than a true battle.

1746

The Battle of Culloden near Inverness, Scotland, is a contender for the last battle on *British* soil. A crushing victory by the Duke of Cumberland's forces ended the Jacobite Rising and the aspirations of Charles Edward Stuart (aka Bonnie Prince Charlie or the Young Pretender), grandson of James II/VII.

1797

The Battle of Fishguard, Wales, was a small, unsuccessful invasion by the Revolutionary French Republic. More of a skirmish than a battle notwithstanding that is was an invasion.

1838

The so-called Battle of Bossenden Wood in Kent was a disturbance caused by a small group of dissident labourers led by an imposter and recent inmate of the Kent County Lunatic Asylum, the self-styled Sir William Courtney. 'Battle' is an exaggerated description of this event. In modern times, it would have been dealt with by the police rather than the military.

1940

On 27 September – again in Kent, this time at Graveney Marsh – a clash took place between a company of the London Irish Rifles led by Captain John Cantopher and the four crew of a downed German Junkers Ju 88. Hardly a skirmish let alone a battle.

1940

The Battle of Britain took place in the skies *over* Britain during the three months and three weeks from 10 July to 31 October. This was a new form of warfare not seen before in the history of Britain or anywhere else and, therefore, not usually listed in the claims to be the last Battle *on* British soil. Let us now put that right.

The Spitfires and Hurricanes of the British and Canadian Air Forces were based *on* the ground *in* Britain; the pilots were current residents *of* Britain; they lived, and sadly many died, *on* British soil during this battle. To them surely must go the 'honour' of the last battle on the soil of the British Isles for, in the apposite words of Winston Churchill:

> *"Never in the field of human conflict was so*
> *much owed by so many to so few."*

Made in the USA
San Bernardino, CA
31 January 2019